Mind Games:

Emotionally Manipulative Tactics Partners Use to Control Relationships and Force the Upper Hand

By Pamela Kole

Table of Contents

Introduction

At one point in my life, I was what you might call a *doormat*. It's not something I'm proud of, but it was an essential part of my identity and it motivated me to become who I am today.

At the height of my doormat phase, I met Mark.

Mark seemed like an amazing catch, and I was honestly a little surprised that he even showed interest in me. Later, I discovered that he had targeted me from afar. I had such low self-esteem that he thought I would be easy to mold into whatever he wanted. I was blissfully unaware of this fact and thought his attentions signaled a turnaround in my life.

He was extremely handsome, came from a great family, and had a lucrative career with a huge upside. What more could I want?

As it turns out, just to be treated with the **respect and courtesy** that any member of the human race expects as a given.

The first three months we were together were among the happiest of my life, as he told me everything that I ever wanted to hear from a boyfriend. He told me I was the best thing to happen to him and I honestly believed he was the best thing to ever happen to me.

Gradually and slowly, things began to change. He began to act more irritable and short with me. He grew angry at the drop of a hat. He began nitpicking at my choices in daily life and even dictated what I was allowed to wear on certain days. He started initiating arguments where it seemed the only logical answer was that I was somehow always at fault.

I would complain to my friends, but when they suggested that Mark was the obvious problem, I was able to rationalize their reasons away instantly. *He's just tired, in a bad mood, touchy about that one subject...*

I realized at some point that I was profoundly unhappy in the relationship on a daily basis and I had never felt worse about myself and my self-worth... but I was deathly afraid of Mark leaving me. He had beaten my self-esteem so far down that I thought I wasn't deserving of better treatment, and that no one else would accept or love me again besides him. I couldn't leave my apartment without telling him exactly where I was going, with whom, and when I would be back. I had a curfew and a dress code.

I felt he was the best thing my life because I was told that I was a terrible person every day.

This was classic, almost **textbook emotional manipulation**. Mark sure knew how to play me.

It took a series of interventions from my friends for me to realize what was truly happening and break my own beliefs surrounding it. Unfortunately, this was two years in, and I was only a husk of the person I was before I met Mark. I felt like I couldn't leave him because who would have me in my weakened and pathetic state?

Does any of this sound familiar?

Don't let yourself fall prey to the same pitfalls I did. You're worth more than that, and no one should ever possess that kind of power over you, especially if they're going to use it to beat you down and control you.

Don't fool yourself into thinking that this can't happen to you. It can, will, and does every day to people just like you. Strong people, and people you would never expect. Emotional manipulation doesn't discriminate by gender, culture, or race.

Don't let someone else's lack of perspective on healthy relationships and insecurities affect yours.

One. Why Do They Hurt You?

Emotional manipulation is abuse of the highest degree. Make no mistake about it. Mind games are motivated by malice, whether they realize it or not.

At the most basic level, abuse is simply treating someone or something in an unfair and harmful fashion. Just because you may not have been physically injured or even touched doesn't mean that it doesn't deserve to be called abuse. In fact, that's one of the pitfalls of dealing with emotional manipulation and abuse – the absence of a physical scar does not excuse behavior, nor mean that you are not being damaged mentally.

And the payoff for abusers is so petty that it's befuddling to understand why they engage in all of their mind games.

To an abuser, emotional manipulation serves one goal and one goal only. It's the determination to *win* and possess the most power in a relationship. They believe that when they have such power, they will be happy... and it's all at your expense. Again, they might not realize their motives, but their actions will prove easier to interpret.

It's an amazingly unhealthy approach to a relationship, and anything for that matter. If you approach something solely to win, that means you put winning as a higher priority than someone's feelings and ultimately wellbeing.

If you approach an argument solely to win, then you ignore the underlying issues and are not resolution-focused. And if you approach a relationship solely to win, then you are spitting on the underlying concept of a relationship.

You are mistaking it for a battle of vulnerability and control, while relationships should be the polar opposite. Relationships are a give-and-take and require compromise. Relationships are not a zero-sum game, and they do not function like a dom-sub relationship from the BDSM world. Abusers forget this, or worse... they realize it and know exactly what they are doing when they manipulate you.

Abusers embody a frightening combination of traits that make them dangerous.

They are focused and intentional about what they want from you. They have a penchant for deception and backhanded tactics of questionable morality. They view relationships as power struggles and always want to be on the winning side of it. They have impaired consciences and don't mind fighting dirty. They can lie with a straight face and have a professional-level poker face – perhaps because they believe themselves and are able to tune out any negative feedback or criticism as "not their fault."

They live in a zone of danger where they are smart enough to be able to fool you yet obtuse enough to not see the damage they are doing.

The list goes on… and so will your relationship unless you are able to catch these sneaky, manipulative maneuvers that can occur on a daily basis.

The thing about abusers is that along with power, they only recognize a relationship that is 100% on their own terms. They don't have any experience with a relationship of compromise or mutual solutions… or they are just selfish enough to make sure that they aren't in one. I'm not sure which is worse, but in either case, it is clear that they have no interest in treating you well.

But let's get one thing straight.

Your abuser wants power over you, and this means one simple truth.

They don't love you.

They just don't, or else they would treat you better and respect you. They may think they love you, but that's a testament to their skewed understanding of love and how relationships work. At best, they believe they know what's best for you and seek to control every aspect of your life.

If they don't love you, what do they love? What motivates them?

They love controlling someone.

They love living on only their terms. That's what gives them pleasure, and they will go to any lengths to maintain that pleasure. That's why they make you feel downtrodden on a daily basis and constantly tell you that you aren't good enough or smart enough. You hear it so much, you begin believing it instead of trusting yourself and your self-esteem... and that's exactly where your abuser wants you. It makes them feel better about themselves and happy to be adored.

That's why they'll put you on the defensive and attack you instead of admitting their own flaws and mistakes. When they react emotionally instead of rationally, it's another form of control they exhibit over you. That's why they'll push and pull you emotionally until you can't take it anymore and fear losing them so much that you'll act however they want just to keep them around. They might not always realize that they're doing it, but the lack of intention doesn't decrease the impact.

Emotional manipulation is not just a simple mind game — it is abusive and psychologically scarring. Recognizing what your abuser's goals and weapons are is a huge part of the battle, and that's what I hope to arm you with in this book. Battle against your abuser's insecurities and lack of understanding of healthy relationships to seize the respect that you deserve.

Insecurities can fuel nightmares that even your abusers are unaware of.

Two. Red Flags And Signs of Emotional Manipulation

Emotional manipulation is rarely as direct and obvious as you might think. Perhaps it might be obvious to the casual bystander, but when you're **emotionally invested**, everything simply appears incredibly complex and layered.

That's why it appears so easy for us to dissect, analyze, and help with the relationship issues of our friends. We see how people are affected by large issues that are often deal breakers – and we gloss over the smaller details that people will use to justify their actions that simply don't matter. We can't do this to ourselves.

There is a reasonable explanation for every negative action and statement that makes you think that it was justified and you deserved it somehow. You can explain everything away and make it acceptable. They may have acted this way, but there are so many factors involved... Or are there?

That's the first sign that you're being emotionally manipulated and controlled by your abuser. You are able to **rationalize** your abuser's actions to yourself, to make it seem like they are logical and justified. What they said or did wasn't really so bad because you deserved it... right?

It's a slow process that makes you a master of mental gymnastics to justify your abuser's actions. They have shrunk your self-esteem and made you feel stupid and useless on a daily basis. They have attacked you emotionally and verbally until you can't muster the effort to defend yourself anymore. They have disclaimed all responsibility and make it clear that you are to blame for all shortcomings in the relationship.

Eventually, you start to believe everything that you're told, and you're stuck trying to explain to yourself why you continue to accept such treatment. You rationalize. Every act your abuser commits has a reason, and that reason is a shortcoming of yours.

You feel the need to walk on **eggshells** around your abuser, for fear of them lashing out at you for something you're not quite sure you are actually responsible for. Nonetheless, they will convince you that you are. Your abuser always seems upset and annoyed with you, and you don't feel like you know how to make them happy.

Consequently, you are always beset by a sense of guilt and gloom in your relationship. What have you done wrong lately, and what is the next thing you will have to apologize for?

The worst part is that you can never express these negative feelings of displeasure because they'll just bring up your own shortcomings and condition you to avoid confrontation and allowing you to express yourself. Your on-going issues never get resolved. You are always on the defensive. You are never quite sure if your abuser is angry with you, and never quite sure **where you stand** with them.

You unknowingly become a doormat of epic proportions.

As a result of all of the above, you feel inadequate and your self-esteem shrinks by the day. Surely you can't be happy in this relationship... **yet** you've started to believe that you aren't worthy of happiness, so you don't want to mess up your relationship because it still might be the best thing to ever happen to you.

This is a very heavily studied phenomenon known as the cycle of abuse.

When an abuser abuses too heavily, the abused retreats in desperation. The abuser makes heavy amends and promises to be different, thus luring the abused back in with the love so craved. Each outburst is characterized as a one-time occurrence. Cue

the next transgression and the cycle repeats
itself endlessly.

In one phrase, you know you're being
emotionally manipulated if your joy at finding
love has slowly turned into the fear and anxiety
of losing it.

Three. The Mind Games

1. Occasional approval.

Occasional approval is exactly what it sounds like. You can do the greatest things in the world for your partner, and they will only acknowledge it and show approval and affection occasionally.

It doesn't matter what you do. They have made a concerted effort to only show you a certain amount of approval – a quota of sorts – to keep you under their power. They keep you under their thumb to keep you reaching for approval and feeling negatively about yourself.

Many psychological studies have shown that being positively reinforced on an inconsistent basis is addicting and keeps people coming back. It's the entire basis for **gambling** – if you won every time you pulled the slot, you would have no incentive to keep trying and coming back. Instead, you stay glued to the slot machine, and you're not even sure why.

Your partner knows this instinctually, and thus doesn't reward your every positive action like they should. It keeps you searching for their approval, which is the equivalent of the jackpot at the slot machine. You may even become **obsessed** with their approval and it may consume you. This is not uncommon, and can drive you to anxiety. In the end, it ultimately makes you fear being left by them, so you keep trying harder and harder to win their approval.

It's a cycle that doesn't end easily, and is only designed to benefit your partner and the amount of power he/she holds over you.

Example: You've cooked your partner dinner from scratch every night of the week. They only really thank, acknowledge, and praise you one of the nights. This makes you think that the food the other nights was inadequate, and just makes you try harder to cook better each subsequent time to gain that praise you desire.

Consequence: You enjoy the attention they give you occasionally so much that it's like hitting an oasis in the desert. You may become obsessed with their approval and keep working towards it, creating an incredibly unbalanced relationship.

2. The disguised putdown.

This isn't a book about obvious red flags – there would be no point to that and you probably wouldn't need someone to tell you about them.

This is a book about the sneaky, underhanded, and plain dirty tricks that abusers use against you that you might not catch otherwise!

That's exactly what the disguised putdown is.

A normal putdown is, "Wow, you're really bad at that" to your face. A **disguised** putdown is couched under the pretense of another purpose, making a negative statement 'acceptable.'

It can be disguised as an innocent question, teaching, advice, helping, or offering solutions, but the end result is that you are putdown and insulted by a negative statement.

Your abuser knows that their hold on you depends on how superior they feel, and also how inferior you feel. They make it a point to demean and put you down at every chance possible to keep this power balance in their favor. Sometimes they are clever about it, such as with the disguised putdown.

This way, it makes it seem like their **intentions** are positive and caring, despite the end result of you feeling terrible about yourself. That may be how they justify it to themselves. Your abuser is a master of emotional manipulation and knows just what makes you tick – make no mistake, this Is intentionally hurtful. It often comes from a place of condescension, to make matters even worse.

Example: Them: "Hey, you really need to work on your listening skills. You're such a terrible listener. Why don't you check out a book called _____, it will help people like you. You're welcome!"

Consequence: Even though the suggestion appears to be helpful and well-intentioned, you feel insulted and your self-esteem is lowered as a result. Maybe you ARE a bad listener. What else are you bad at? You can be sure that they will point it out.

3. Gaslighting.

Unfortunately, gaslighting is a widely-practiced phenomenon that you yourself might have used from time to time.

Nothing to the extent that your abuser does, but it can be very easy to fall into gaslighting mode if you're not careful. This doesn't make it right, however.

Gaslighting is when you bring an issue up to your abuser, but they immediately **invalidate it** and proclaim that the only problem is with you.

You can see how powerful this might be, as it allows the abuser to deflect all issues about their own actions and focus instead of something that is irrelevant. They do briefly acknowledge it, but deflect it all the same.

It's also a strong refusal to accept responsibility in any form, which your abuser prefers because it means that the responsibility falls upon you.

When the focus of a problem is shifted back onto you, the conversation branches off into all of your shortcomings, which decreases your self-esteem. Most importantly, the focus is never on the abuser and their actions. You'll start to doubt yourself and conform to the new standards that they have set for you.

This also conditions you to never show your displeasure or bring up issues you have with your abuser, because you know that the end result will be an argument, you feeling poorly about yourself, and you walking away with your tail between your legs having been corrected. Of course, this keeps the power in your abuser's hand, as they have just silenced you effectively without having to do anything.

Finally, gaslighting totally invalidates your concerns and can make you doubt if they are even valid. This can drive you crazy with doubt and anxiety, and make you feel like your abuser is the only one who will ever accept you.

Example:

You: "Why did you say that to my mother? That was so rude!"

Them: "What are you talking about? I was perfectly polite and you both just took it the wrong way. What's wrong with you two? Don't be so emotional. You need serious help and you need to learn how to talk to people."

Consequences: After they say that the issue is with you, the focus will be on you and any of the problems that they choose to bring up – you being emotional or otherwise in the wrong. This means that the original issue will not be addressed, and you are unjustly on the defensive… even when you are in the right.

4. Creating a wedge.

Since your abuser is all about retaining the power and control in your relationship, it's clear that they will do anything necessary to keep it.

Sometimes this can include third parties and using them like **pawns** to short-circuit your insecurities and throw doubt into your mind.

Creating a wedge is when your abuser introduces other people into your relationship and gives them the attention and duties that you should have as their significant other. It doesn't matter if they are men or women – you can be jealous of both, and they are keenly aware of this.

The idea is to make you jealous and cause you to be upset, which increases their power over you. You will feel less and less like a priority, and perhaps that they are even thinking of leaving you. Clearly, this makes you want to hold on and do anything they want in fear of the leaving.

You will never know exactly where you stand with them, and that's a very demoralizing feeling with someone that is supposed to be there for you regardless of the circumstances.

After they have made you insecure enough to cling to them and raise every single insecurity you have, they will comfort you and reassure you that they are with you. And thus your dependency is increased, along with the power they have over you.

Example: They will flirt in front of you with the opposite sex to make you jealous, 100% aware that you are there and watching. If you show displeasure later, they will tell you that your jealousy and insecurity is the problem, while continuing to create wedges with additional people.

Consequence: You grow jealous, and yet you are told that your jealousy is invalid and that you must accept their actions. You start disliking the third party wedge, but you find yourself wanting to draw closer to your abuser, despite knowing that they might be acting inappropriately. You just can't stand their attention going to other people, because you barely get enough positive attention as it is.

5. Snide side comments.

Snide side comments can add serious tinder to a flame. Even if your abuser has nothing but positive things to say at the time, they might sneak in a few snide side comments to completely ruin the positive effect of whatever else they said.

A **snide side comment** undermines the positive content of a statement with a negative, and is disguised as a random thought, observation, musing, or simple wondering.

These comments wear on people when made as frequently as abusers do. Abusers fail to see the positive in actually praising you, and can't do so without making sure to remind you that you are low-value to them. And again, when you continually hear that you are low-value, it's impossible to not start believing it to some degree, and **your self-esteem will take a nosedive**.

Recall that abusers want to win, and they want power in a relationship. Keeping you in your place with a snide and rude side comment accomplishes just that, but it allows them to hide within positivity. They complimented you, they can't tell you the negative aspects as well? They can't tell it like it is?

It doesn't matter to the abuser how they feel superior to you – just that they do, and a side comment is an easy way to put you down.

Example: Them: "Great job on singing that song! You're so great! Now if you could just stay in tune…"

Consequence: Perhaps you pride yourself on your singing, but it doesn't matter that the abuser has said something positive. All you can focus on now is the negative comment they made at the end, poorly hidden as an observation. You start to doubt your singing skills, and your abuser has just lowered your self-esteem.

6. The guilt trip.

Now this is an emotionally manipulative tactic that you're probably familiar with.
Guilt works in the following way – someone wants you to do something, and makes it seem like **you owe them and are obligated to do it**. So you do it, despite not wanting to, and without an actual obligation.

Guilt can operate in many ways in an abusive relationship. If you bring up a concern, they will **play the victim** and guilt you into feeling bad that you said anything to hurt them. If they do something wrong, they will put the blame on you and make you feel guilty for apparently committing a wrong.

If they want you to do something for them, they will make note of all the sacrifices they have made for you, the gestures they have made for you, and any miniscule compliment they have paid you. Your action should be in recognition and repayment of those things. This is ridiculous, when you look at it from an outside perspective.

Yet all the same, **we cannot refuse**. You tell yourself that they care about you, so you should do things for them, even if you don't want to or hate to. Out of guilt and obligation, we do many things, and your abuser is keenly aware of that. They know they you do care about them, and they take advantage of that easily... because that's what they can do when the balance of power in a relationship is incredibly skewed.

They are taking advantage of a perceived emotional debt in the relationship that they alone have created.

Clearly, this decreases your self-esteem and truly confuses your mind. You don't want to do this, but because you love them, you should. After all, isn't love sacrifice and being miserable sometimes? Guilt tripping forces you to act just like someone else wants.

Example: Them: "I can't believe that you aren't going to pick me up from the airport. I do things for you all the time. I bought you that scone. I fixed that closet door. What's wrong with you that you don't prioritize me?"

Consequence: This makes you feel worthless and ungrateful, even though they are completely separate things. They force you into doing something that you may not want to do or even have time to do, and make them your number one priority by phrasing it like your love depends on it. Your love depends on many things, and only the way their power increases depends on it.

7. Judgment and shame.

Judgment is something that we are afraid of on a daily basis, but it shouldn't be something that you're afraid of from **inside** your relationship. After all, isn't the reason this person is with you is because they accept your flaws and think you're a great person anyway? **A relationship is supposed to be almost judgment-free**. But of course an abusive relationship doesn't conform to basic standards or common sense.

Judgment in a relationship functions just like it does outside – if you say something to your abuser, they may deem it 'stupid,' 'worthless,' or 'a waste of time' among other things. It just makes you not want to open up to them or tell them anything you have done, for fear of them deeming you stupid.

As with many of the tactics in this book, this is a power play that your abuser knows will lower your self-esteem. If they put down everything that you like and do, it makes you less enthusiastic about them, and distance yourself from them. Not only does making what you like sound stupid make you want to do them less, it means that you are **getting used to** being persuaded by them and shifting your priorities based on their opinions and statements.

Their power over you grows every time they judge what you do and shame you for it, rightfully or not.

Judgment and shame are black and white, and you will be living according to that person's definition of right and wrong.

The shame and judgment aren't confined to the activity or thing themselves – they make us personally feel unacceptable, inadequate, defective, and plain dumb. Your choices are your own and any partner worth their salt should realize that and respect it, instead of making you feel worthless for them.

Example:

You: "I really like that girl's dress. It's pretty, isn't it?"

Them: "No it's very ugly and too revealing. She's probably a slut. Do you want to be a slut too by dressing that revealing?"

Consequence: Not only is this a refusal of a casual comment that you were making, it's an insult to you. It implies things that you weren't trying to even discuss, and makes a direct attack on your character. This shames you and makes you feel bad about yourself, no matter how untrue it is.

8. You missed the point.

This manipulative maneuver is particularly frustrating because it completely sidesteps what happened, and invalidates your concerns immediately.

Missing the point is as follows: your abuser will say something malicious or negative towards you, and you might retaliate at them or become visibly upset.

Instead of rightfully and gracefully acknowledging your point and emotional hurt, he or she blames you. This time he blames your lack of understanding for your emotional pain, and that though he might have misspoken slightly, it was your misinterpretation that caused the entire issue.

Your abuser disclaims all responsibility for your emotional harm, and essentially is able to sidestep the whole issue. The discussion then becomes about you, and your shortcomings in reading and interpreting your abuser.

Why can't you just listen better and be less stupid as to understand better?

This is clearly not the issue at hand... and even if their intentions were pure, does that matter when harm is done? Your abuser will insist that they didn't mean to hurt you, but that's often a lie. By hurting you, they know that it keeps your inferiority complex alive and self-esteem low.

Missing the point is **reminiscent of gaslighting**, except it uses misdirection to attack instead of a direct attack.

Example:

Them: "That was such a stupid thing you said to my boss, I can't believe you said it. I'm going to be so embarrassed by my thoughtless husband."

You: "Your boss laughed and told me that he really liked me, what do you mean? I thought he really liked me."

Them: "Oh yeah…. He did. I just mean that you should be careful about what you say. Didn't you hear me? You missed the point. You're so sensitive."

Consequence: They directly insulted you and avoided the consequences of it by framing it as your issue. They get off scot-free, while you are left wondering whether you are indeed a bad listener, or sensitive. It causes self-doubt and allows the abuser to say essentially whatever they want, whenever they want.

9. Words of affirmation.

If you haven't noticed by now, abusers take advantage of cycles of love and hate.

They do something to disparage you and make you hate them, but at the same time, there's something that makes you love them and want to stay with them. Often, this love is actually misguided security and low self-esteem.

Sometimes, it is a **one-way, non-mutual love** that is created by the abuser's words of affirmation.

Words of affirmation are just what you want to hear from your significant other – that they love you, how important you are to them, they are sorry, and how they will never hurt you again. Only thing is – you never hear these things from them unless you are extremely upset and threatening to walk away. Or they feel the need to exert their power over you in some way. It could be when you've reached your boiling point, but these words of affirmation are what your abuser knows will get you to stop being angry and stay.

Unfortunately, this probably isn't a true feeling of love or respect. It's just giving you what you want to hear and will calm you down – **that's just appeasement, not love**.

Abusers know how to turn the charm on – after all, they are master manipulators of people and know just what to say to make people like or believe them.

Even when you're angry, you are still vulnerable to these sweet words of affirmation, and they completely knock you off your guard so the abuser doesn't have to face any consequences. They make you vulnerable and sentimental, which weakens your resolve about whatever you are upset about.

Just remember, this isn't love. They love dominating and controlling you, not you.

Example:

You: "I've had it! I need to really think about this relationship. Give me some time."

Them: "What are you talking about? I didn't mean any of that and I love you so much. How could you do this to me, no one will ever love you like I do!"

Consequence: There's a lot going on here. Your abuser completely rebuffs your concern and makes it about them as a victim. Your issue goes unnoticed and unaddressed. They break out the big guns with a phrase that you probably yearn to hear, which catches you off guard and makes you vulnerable to sentiment. Finally, it makes you ask if you are even worthy of their love.

10. Altered reality.

Each of our realities are relative based on our personal experiences and memories. You are completely entitled to your interpretation of that reality, and you alone are best equipped to talk about it.

However, abusers cannot allow this to happen for two reasons.

First, it would expose them for all the devious tricks and tactics they use to maintain control over you. This would be devastating to them, as you would see that they are intentionally attempting to gain control over you and manipulate you.

Second, it means that the abusers would have to live in the same reality as you, and that would objectively make them terrible people. They might not like seeing this about themselves.

So what do abusers do?

Abusers alter your reality, which makes them appear more favorable to you. It's also a reality where you are the screw up, you don't understand them, and they are the best thing that will ever happen to you. It's scary if you step back and think about it, but that's the world your abuser prefers to live in.

They alter your reality by making you doubt yourself, denying what they said or did, remembering false and wrong stories, and invalidating your opinion and memories. It literally distorts your reality to the point where you don't know what's real or not, and you eventually bend to their reality. It breeds self-doubt, and can even make you feel like you're taking crazy pills – but then your abuser assures that that they are right and you are wrong, so what can you do?

Another variation of this is **selectively forgetting promises** and important things... basically, things and events that benefit you and are a hassle or chore to them.

Finally, of course the altered reality includes **direct lying**. Abuser will do anything to get the results they want, and they don't care if there are repercussions for anyone but themselves.

This is all a tactic to get their way, at the expense of your sanity and reality.

Example:

You: "You promised to take me to the opera last week! You promised that we would have great seats and it would be an amazing night out."

Them: "No, I absolutely didn't. You must have misheard me. Are you crazy? Why would I promise that – you know I hate the opera. You completely misunderstood me, I was probably just making a joke. Get it together."

Consequence: You have just been completely dismissed and turned aside. Even though they probably did promise to take you to the opera, it doesn't matter now. That's not the issue – the issue is now your faulty memory, and that's where the discussion and argument will focus on. Over time, you begin to actually question your memory, and blindly listen to your abuser as always correct. This is a dangerous slippery slope.

11. Trivializing.

One of the worst things anyone can do to you is tell you that your problem really isn't a problem.

It just makes no sense. Of course it's a problem – you feel poorly about it, and it's affecting you. It's like **denying that someone's favorite color is blue** – who are you to tell them that, and how would you even know?

That is exactly what trivializing does.

Your abuser trivializes any problem or issue you have into something small, and essentially tells you that your problem isn't a problem. They tell you that you're wrong, your opinion is wrong, and most importantly, they aren't at fault for anything.

Trivializing is when your abuser takes your mountain and makes it into a molehill. It's incredibly dismissive, disrespectful, and the opposite of empathy. **Empathy** should be a cornerstone in any relationship, even friendship, and it just signals that basic human decency and common sense are missing from yours.

What trivializing does is make a problem that you have with him... into a problem about yourself. You're overreacting, they'll say. You're taking it too seriously and can't take a joke, they'll say. It's not a big deal. Who cares anyway in the grand scheme of it all?

Your problem is only a problem because you're whining about it. Stop whining.

These are all **cop out answers** from your abuser that results in one conclusion: they don't have to own up to anything they've done wrong if they can convince you that you are the one who's wrong, or is making a big deal out of nothing. This is manipulation at its finest, and leads to you feeling dramatic, downtrodden, and unworthy of your abuser. Perfect for them – they win on all fronts.

Example:

You: "Why do you keep making fun of me in front of your friends? It's really embarrassing for me, and it makes me feel really stupid."

Them: "What are you talking about? They all love you. You're making a big deal out of nothing. Can't you take a joke? Where's your sense of humor?"

Consequence: As you can see, the fault is just piled onto you. It doesn't matter that the only thing you did wrong was have feelings of some sort. Your abuser takes zero accountability and responsibility for their actions, and you get left holding the short end of the stick. Your problems will go unsolved, and they will continue to act negatively.

12. The silent treatment.

The silent treatment is as disrespectful as it is frustrating.

It's **emotional blackmail**.

Back when we were children, one of our best methods of solving arguments was simply to walk away and turn our backs. Unfortunately, some people, namely your abuser, still think that this is a valid way of resolving problems.

The silent treatment is when your abuser **refuses to communicate** with you when they perceive that you have done something wrong, or just want to convey their displeasure to you. They're almost never correct when they think you've done something wrong, and it's a completely arbitrary and subjective standard they live by.

Unfortunately, that just doesn't matter to you sometimes. The silent treatment and cold shoulder are a **punishment**, and you just don't want to keep being punished and ignored. It's extremely painful to be ignored by someone that you think you love, and at some point, you don't even care if you're completely innocent. You just want the pain to end, so you apologize and attempt to make it up to them.

This plays just into their hands.

Like the petulant and angry child who sits in the corner out of anger, so does your abuser to get what they want. You cave because you're bigger than that, and you choose to take the high road. All the while, this ignores any semblance of communication, and actually discourages it. What kind of communication can you have with a wall? It's not about communication to your abuser – it's about power, control, and a power struggle that they must win.

And because you just want to end the hurtful silence, you acquiesce and give in. What's really being communicated is that you just aren't that important to them, and that you aren't worth their time or love. You feel powerless and betrayed.

There are variations of the silent treatment — whenever your abuser does something negative, and you must comply with their demand to make them stop. You can use your imagination for this one.

Example: Your partner/abuser stops responding to you because they perceive that you slighted them in front of their friends at a party earlier.

Consequence: You can't communicate or even talk to them about what they thought the problem was because they won't comply with you. This frustrates you, and to even begin solving the issue, you must apologize and volunteer responsibility for whatever the slight was. You are in a constant pattern of apologizing and trying to read their mind.

13. You're not perfect, either!

Abusers are some of the biggest **nitpickers** in the world, way bigger than both of your overbearing parents combined.

This is because their manipulation has one ultimate goal, and that goal is **power and control over you**. Even if you're perfect, they would find something to nitpick about you because that devalues you and lowers your self-esteem. There's a threshold of self-esteem where you begin viewing your abuser as your savior and the best thing to ever happen to you, and this is their constant aim – to keep you below that threshold.

It's despicable.

Constant nitpicking is designed to destroy your self-esteem and make it so that your mood is always low and you have nothing to feel good about. Abusers turn you into prey, and they're the predator whenever they can be. And when you're the prey, the predator can toy with it as long as they want, however they want. Remember, it's all about control and dominance, a game that shouldn't exist in a relationship.

When your self-esteem is low enough, you'll eventually fear losing your abuser even if they were the one who put you down there.

There's nothing any other partner would find remotely attractive or interesting about you, so you might as well stay in the current situation. You won't be able to do any better.

Example:

You: "Why don't you ever pay attention to me when we're out with your friends? You know I don't like hanging out with them that much, but you always leave me completely alone when we're out."

Them: "Well what about you? You're not perfect! You always forget my birthday and last year you didn't even get me anything. And I pay for your dinner whenever we go out with my friends, you never pay me back either."

Consequence: Your initial concern is completely sidestepped and deflected. All that matters it the flaws that you have, that may or may not be true, and which are definitely unrelated to the issue that you brought up. It's a not-so-subtle way to turning attention to nitpicking you, and what your imperfections and flaws are. Amazingly, it also manages to trivialize your concern. You are now on the defensive, and they get away free.

14. It wasn't me.

Abusers live in an interesting world. It's like they're **royalty** in their minds.

Nothing they do has consequences, and they are never responsible for anyone feeling negatively. Further, they are always the hero or victim of a story, and others are always the ones who have wronged or insulted them. They are always justified, rational, and kind to a fault. A modern day **Gatsby**.

Pure fantasy, of course.

This is a mindset that enables a host of behaviors that your abuser employs on a daily basis because there is a complete lack of accountability. Most notably, nothing is ever their fault.

If you think it's their fault, it's actually yours. Or you've misinterpreted. Or it's circumstantial. Or it's a third party's fault. Or... it's your fault.

Whatever the consequence or penalties arising from their actions, your abusers will do their damndest to deny any responsibility. Naturally, the blame has to fall somewhere, and they know that eventually the blame will fall onto your shoulders.

This is perfect, because then your abuser can guilt you about something, and twist their own actions into consequences from your actions. So not only are you the cause of the problem apparently, you are now being vilified for it. There's no sympathy, empathy, or understanding from your abuser.

They know to take the focus off of them, they must blame and guilt you to the highest degree. And subsequently, all of the little failures and arguments in your relationship will become your fault. After all, if they keep saying it, it's got to be true... right?

Example:

You: "Why did you have to be so mean to that walter? He's just doing his job."

Them: "What do you mean? If he was doing his job I wouldn't have any reason to be mean to him. Besides, if you had asked him properly for the water, there would be no issue. It's not my fault."

Consequence: Even though it is 100% their action, and no one forced them to be mean to the waiter, the abuser disclaims all responsibility and attempts to pawn the blame off on you, the waiter, and circumstances. It's almost devoid of logic.

15. Setting a smokescreen.

A smokescreen in normal terms is something that acts to conceal the true nature or intent of something else.

In an abuser's vocabulary, a **smokescreen** is something they use to avoid and escape questions that hit too close to home.

Even if your abuser has ultimate power over you, it's likely that you've brought your concerns up to them before. After all, they care about you, right? They should want to remedy the situation and smooth matters over.

That's not their motivation, however.

They may want to make you THINK that they want it, but their end goal is always power and control over you. They know that having to truly answer many of the tough questions you would ask them about their feelings for you would destroy their power over you, so they simply avoid it.

They throw a smokescreen over it and use another issue as a diversion. Sometimes this might just be a topic change or deflection, which changes the focus of a discussion to a tangent. If you really want to talk about the issue that's bothering you, you'll have to continually bring it up, and we all know it was a big obstacle to bring it up the first time.

A stronger smokescreen and diversion is bringing up a problem they have with you, so also be prepared to see that. This successfully allows the abuser to avoid the issue and continue their negative actions.

Example:

You: "Hey, why do you always ignore me when I say that I don't want to have sex?"

Them: "Sex? Last night, Conan was on and was talking about that... he had a pretty funny joke about it. Besides, I don't complain when you forget to wash the dishes, now do I?

Consequence: This is a classic smokescreen. They barely address the issue of forcing sex, and the conversation is driven to another topic. Your concern goes unnoticed, and you just feel unheard and ultimately dismissed. The conversation trajectory is then probably about his complaint about the dishes, conditioning you to not bring up your concerns with him for fear of being attacked back.

16. Trojan horse.

In most cases, a confidant serves an extremely important role. It's someone that you can tell your secrets to and lean on in tough times when you need support and help.

Your abuser takes advantage of the fact that you will lean on them. The more you rely on them, the more power and control they hold over you, and the closer they are to their goal of dominating you. So what's a Trojan horse as a confidant?

A Trojan horse is a confidant who discloses extremely intimate knowledge and details about their personal life.

This is to emulate a false sense of closeness and intimacy... because if they told you about their mother's breast cancer, you must be extremely close and comfortable with them. The mere fact that they have told you this knowledge suggests that you are close, and your abuser preys on that knowledge.

So when you feel close and intimate with someone, you open up to them yourself and become increasingly more vulnerable to them. **Your guards are lowered**. They have successfully Trojan-horsed into your heart and mind, and that is exactly where they want to be so they can control you most effectively. Being a forced confidant and opening up to you prematurely is the fastest way to your soul, and it's often an intentional series of disclosures.

In another sense, this is **pure seduction**. Your abuser knows what will get you to open up to them so they can get close to you.

Example: Your abuser repeatedly tells you about their family situation, how their father walked out, and how their mother dated a revolving door of criminals and drug addicts. They may cry occasionally, and swear that they don't open up to anyone like this, but that there's something special about you.

Consequence: This makes you feel quite special and wanted by them. If they can trust you with their personal information, then you must be able to trust them with yours. You open up to them and reveal your insecurities and vulnerabilities, which is just what your abuser wants.

17. The time machine.

Abusers are masterful in many ways. One of the ways is that they're smart enough to essentially invent time machines when they need them, and completely dispose of them when they don't.

A time machine for an abuser is when they reach into the past and continually bring up any mistakes or negative actions that you've committed, and continue to hold it over you even if it was 100% resolved and over with. They'll bring up that one act from 5 years ago, even if it's unrelated to the issue at hand, and continually hammer you with it, as if that makes their transgressions more acceptable.

The reason your abuser does this is to obscure the sins they have committed presently. It's a re-phrasing of, "Hey, you're not perfect either!" Except it draws exclusively from the past on matters that have since closed. This is because there probably isn't anything logical your abuser can do to distract from their actions, so they must dig into the past to find something big enough that will be adequate.

And of course, after your abuser brings out their time machine, hops in, and re-emerges with a problem with the past, the focus is on the past. There is no more discussion about what happened yesterday, and you are suddenly on the defensive and they are on the offensive... which is a role that they cherish.

Example:

You: "Can you clean up the garage like you promised 4 months ago?"

Them: "Remember when you said you'd clean our bathroom for a month and never did it? You're so much worse than me, so don't worry about it. You're really slow."

Consequence: In one brilliant step, your abuser sidesteps, dismisses, and attacks you. This bathroom issue has no relevance to the garage, and makes it clear that the abuser is only concerned with winning and getting his own way.

18. I didn't know!

What's worse – ignorantly committing a crime, or knowingly committing a crime? How about knowingly committing a crime while pretending to be ignorant?

And that's what we have with this emotionally manipulative maneuver. It's when an abuser feigns confusion and ignorance as to what you are talking about, or the consequences of their actions.

"I had no idea that would happen!" "I have no idea what you are talking about." "This is the first I've heard of this." "Since when does that happen from that?"

This has the powerful benefit of taking all responsibility off of the abuser and his actions, and makes a plea based on their supposedly positive intentions. Your abuser wants you to always know that their intentions are positive, and they are only thinking of you for them. This makes you feel **grateful** towards them, even though every act that follows the supposedly positive intentions is hurtful or harmful.

It makes you feel regretful and apologetic for having snapped at them.

Playing dumb or ignorant also tends to confuse you, and even make you doubt the accuracy of your own perception. When you don't feel like you can trust yourself, that's exactly where an abuser wants you and wants to step in to be the one that you can trust... to your detriment. It's in your weakness that your abuser finds a home.

The worst part is possibly that the abuser places their ignorance above your genuine pain and hurt as if that were to mend it.

Example:

You: "How could you yell at me about my weight? You know that I'm super sensitive about it and used to have an eating disorder."

Them: "You never told me that. How was I supposed to know. I thought I was doing you a favor. Why don't you tell me more things about you?"

Consequence: Does it even matter to your abuser that you are sensitive about such issues? There is no apology and no remorse. Suddenly it's your fault that you didn't disclose every possible piece of information about yourself that you might be sensitive about... even if you already have.

19. Well, what about you?

This is a variation on another maneuver, but distinct in what it focuses on. This is when your abuser turns the tables and replaces an issue that you are complaining about with an issue about your shortcomings. This makes your abuser the victim, and subtly makes you to blame for their negative act.

It's a pure ad hominem attack that avoids the issue, and makes it clear that the relationship is about a tit for tat tradeoff and victory for your abuser. If they are caught red-handed, they must call you out as well to attempt to take the attention off of their flaws.

If you complain, they complain about you, and somehow that makes it okay and even. They might even rewrite history to make you at fault.

It's as if two wrongs make a right – if you're wrong about something completely unrelated, that makes them not at fault. This is of course completely illogical, but when your abuser attacks you in a personal way, logic can often fly out the door.

Example:

You: "Why can't you just be more reliable and not flake on me as much? I never know if I'm going to see you and it messes up my schedule."

Them: "Well, what about you? You never clean when you say you're going to and it messes up my schedule. And you always drag me out to shop with you even though you know I don't like it."

Consequence: The abuser doesn't even attempt to address or acknowledge your concern. It turns into a competition for them – who can make the other person feel worse. The winner doesn't have to answer for their transgressions, and guess what? Your abuser will always win this dark game.

20. Traumatic outburst.

Here's how **phobias** work on a macro level.

You have a traumatic experience with something, and are thus conditioned internally and instinctually to avoid it based on the negative memory of that trauma.

Abusers are keenly aware of this cycle of avoidance, and will use it to their fullest advantage. On a daily basis, they might scowl or bring up your own flaws if you bring up their flaws. But on a macro and relationship-wide level, they might use traumatic outbursts to shock and shame you into submission and never bring something up again.

This outburst will be over the top, excessive, and disproportionate. It may attack you, and it may not. It may address your issue, but it probably won't. Finally, it will absolutely be aggressive. But that doesn't matter. All that matters is that you are shocked by it, and will do anything to avoid that outburst from happening again.

Your abuser will use this smartly to avoid any confrontation or big issue that you want to talk about. The focus will be on the outburst itself, and whatever they say during it... effectively skipping over your actual issue. They will depend on your self-preservation and mental conditioning to avoid confrontation even when it's for your own good... based on the strength and ridiculousness of their outburst.

They wield their traumatic outburst like a weapon against you.

Example:

You: "Why can't you and my mother seem to get along? I just don't understand why you can't respect her and let her be a mother to me."

Them: "What the fuck are you talking about? If she was a better mother she'd have raised you better with better manners. She's a terrible mom. Never talk to me about this again. Talking about family. So fucking stupid. I've got enough problems of my own than to worry about your godamn mother. What's her problem? Tell her to go fuck herself."

Consequence: How can you even reply to something like that? You can't really. So you don't. And thus your mother gets swept under the rug forever, as you don't want to incur the wrath of another outburst like that.

21. Belittling your opinions.

There are two truths about opinions. **First**, everyone has one. Deep down, they might not want to say it, but they have an opinion and lean one way or the other. **Second**, no opinion is ever wrong.

That's definitely worth repeating here, because I'm willing to bet that it's a concept that your abuser is not familiar with.

No one's opinions are wrong, and everyone is entitled to feel how they do.

But in your abuser's world, there is only their opinion – everyone else is simply wrong. They judge them to be wrong, stupid, and of low value. And this is precisely what happens to you on a daily basis.

You'll give your opinion on something, and they'll immediately belittle it, judge it, and deem it to be wrong. They'll do this in subtle ways, such as sarcasm, eye rolls, or scoffs, and not so subtle ways, such as literally telling you how stupid you can be. Verbally or non-verbally, it doesn't matter – the clear message is you are only allowed to have an opinion if you agree with your abuser, who is far **smarter** than you.

The end result is a continuous series of blows to your self-esteem, where you begin to blindly listen to your abuser and look to them for guidance on every little thing. You become increasingly more dependent on them as a result of your self-esteem shrinking. It has the added bonus of making you less and less willing to voice your opinions and ideas in the future, which is helpful for your abuser's sense of control and domination.

Example:

You: "I thought that movie was pretty good! I liked the characters and was just entertained the whole time."

Them: "Are you kidding me? I almost made us walk out in the middle. That was so terrible. What are you talking about? You have terrible taste in movies, ugh. You're so wrong."

Consequence: Your opinion gets dismissed right off the bat as stupid and worthless. What's your response to this? It's tough to have a retort to something that belittles you like that. Soon, you'll stop expressing your opinions and start walking on eggshells around your partner because of the negative reactions you always get – and no one wants to feel that way on a regular basis.

22. Playing the poor victim.

Playing the victim is unfortunately something that you are intimately familiar with at this point, though it can manifest in multiple ways. I'll focus on the two main ways in this tactic.

First, if you were to actually bring something up to your abuser – a concern, worry, or suggestion about how they treat you – they would make it all about you. Every act of theirs is contingent on past acts you've committed against them, and they are just trying to cope with your actions.

They are a victim of something you've done - this can come out of nowhere, and your abuser will often focus on actions that have no relation to the present issue, or are seemingly at random... and this may very well be the case, because they are simply grasping for something to defend themselves with.

Of course, this again puts you on the defensive, which is a position that you are familiar with and that they enjoy. Your abuser feels their best when they are making you feel bad about yourself, and acting as a victim is a great way that gives you guilt, remorse, and takes the focus off of them. In their minds, nothing is ever their fault and they are always at someone else's whim, despite this being the opposite case in real life.

The victim complex is a very real thing, so you might be surprised to learn that your abuser truly believes them to be a victim in each dogpile they find themselves in... despite them being the one common thread throughout.

Second, your abuser will expertly play the victim by acting as if an issue you brought up to them has deeply wounded and offended them. As if it's a dagger to the heart that you think they treat you badly. As if they were in complete shock that you had any negative feelings, and that your abuser didn't intentionally create some of them.

When your abuser plays the victim this way, it immediately dismisses your emotional hurt and prioritizes theirs, whether or not it is genuine. Poor them. Now instead of being rightfully angry about your issue, you are guilted into pity by them, and you end up taking care of them and reassuring your abuser that you don't actually hate them. Their reaction of shame and sadness will always be over the top and far greater than your initial issue, so you can't help but pay attention to it and focus on it. They make you feel sorry for them.

Worse yet, your abuser will take this victim mentality outside the confines of your relationship and make others feel sorry for them as well. They will spin the story however they want, and despite how in the right you are, his friends and acquaintances will begin to view you as the bad one.

Abusers are very image-conscious.

To you, they want to appear smarter and more superior. To the public, they want to appear like an ideal partner that others should be jealous of. If anything goes wrong, it's never their fault because they are an amazing partner. There's a large element of self-righteousness, because they project that they are doing their best, and others let them down constantly.

Example:

You: "Why do you always insult me in front of your friends? It makes me feel like you don't care about me and think I'm stupid."

Them: "What do you mean? You call me stupid sometimes too! And you know I'm super sensitive about that. Why do you do that? You make me feel so terrible sometimes."

Them: "I make you feel stupid? Oh my God, I'm so sorry. I feel so terrible. I'm a terrible person. I can't even imagine how you feel. Why am I like this? I can't believe I do this to you. I'm so stupid."

Consequence: In either case, the attention is conveniently off of your issues. In the first instance, the attention turns into an attack on you. In the second instance, the attention turns into an attack on themselves, which begs you to reassure them and take pity on them.

23. You asked for it.

You'll hear this commonly with rape apologists. An innocent woman, walking down the street at night, deserved to be raped because she put herself in that position, dressed provocatively, or said "no" when it really meant "yes."

Clearly a delusional notion that just because a woman is in the wrong place at the wrong time that she deserves to be harmed.

This is known as blaming the victim. Telling people that they were wrong for the harm that they suffered, and that their actions led to it... and what happened after was just an unstoppable consequence when in reality the abuser made many independent choices to continue abusing you in various ways. It again puts your own unhappiness into your own hands, and implies that you would be happier if you didn't act poorly. The burden of shaping up is on you, and never your abuser who is the actual actor.

More importantly, it puts you on the defensive, and make the aggressor (your abuser) innocent. It shifts the responsibility to the wrong party, and doesn't allow for the fact that people should just be decent and not fight fire with fire whenever possible.

Example:

You: "Stop yelling at me when I drive, it's really stressful and doesn't make us get places any faster."

Them: "I wouldn't have to if you weren't such a bad driver. Remember that crash you got into? You're asking for it, and you need someone to help you drive. You can't park either."

Consequence: Your abuser points out reasons they think that justifies their negative statements and actions. This is victim blaming at its finest – because you may have a shortcoming, that you deserve something negative. That it's your fault that you're receiving that kind of treatment.

24. Everything can be rationalized.

Excuses can work in two ways. Your abuser can have excuses for themselves… but you can also be so brainwashed and perspective-less that you can make excuses for them.

As I've discussed before, this is your abuser taking the responsibility of action off of themselves.

If you find yourself making excuses for them, this is a glaringly red flag that you have had your self-esteem lowered enough to the point where you deem such treatment acceptable, and that you don't deserve any better.

That's the reason so many of these of the emotionally manipulative maneuvers in this book even work in the first place. They may not work the first time, but when you combine all of these on a daily basis, your self-esteem and self-valuation just plummet until you feel like your abuser is your savior. It is a very intense cumulative effect.

Example:

You: "Oh, they're just having a bad day, it's fine that they yelled."

You: "I know they're under a lot of stress at work so I should have just left him alone on our anniversary."

You: "I should have known better than to complain about his yelling, it's just how he is and he won't change."

Four. So why do you stay?

Even if you can clearly recognize all of the underhanded emotionally manipulative maneuvers I've presented in this book, it still doesn't mean that leaving your abuser is an easy choice.

You still view yourself as a complex exception where they really do love you, and they just don't know how to express it in a healthy way.

But just imagine the advice you'd give a friend if they came to you with the same set of facts and experiences. The love doesn't matter; only the treatment and impact do.

There are a multitude of reasons to maintain the status quo and most of them are predicated on how low your abuser has made you feel. With your self-esteem at an all-time low, you aren't in conquer the world mode.

You're in hide from the world mode.

Manipulation is a very slow process that is also very gradual. It's often tough to spot big incidents that you can label as abusive, and even tougher when your abuser refuses to label them as negative or admit fault. You are effectively controlled through a mixture of loving and abusive gestures that result in your current position.

It's that lowered self-esteem that makes leaving your abuser a tough decision at the core. If you are told that you are nothing, while your abuser avoids all criticism and flaws, they just look that much more superior to you. They will appear to be the best thing that has ever happened to you, and who wants to give that up willingly? You might even think that they are the only one who will ever accept you, which is obviously a strong motivator to stay.

Some underestimate how happy they can be alone, versus in an unhappy relationship.

With any relationship, there's an element of comfort and security that you're not sure you can find in anyone else. This, of course, is something that everyone has experienced. We also know that it is a supreme lie that never holds true.

Maybe the relationship had an amazing start, and you keep waiting around for what was, versus what the current relationship actually is.

Or further, you yearn for what COULD BE, as opposed to what is. Either case is out of touch with reality... but remember that they were also likely manipulating you at the beginning too, in seducing you and telling you exactly what they wanted you to hear. You might be getting the romantic times, but only in a cycle as a response to over-abusive spells.

You keep holding onto the hope that things will get better, a hope that is supported by your abuser's constant promises.

Maybe you feel that you can't leave because you have a house together, children, or other outside factors beyond your feelings for them that tie you together financially or otherwise.

Maybe you're afraid of judgment from others, and you're deeply embarrassed that you've allowed yourself to be treated this way. Just ask yourself if you'd rather be embarrassed for a few days or suffer at your abuser's hands for a lifetime. People are more understanding of abuse victims than you might expect.

This will be the toughest decision you will ever have to make, but a key element to putting your foot down and leaving is the realization that **you cannot change them**. They will not change for you, and nothing you can do will make them change for the better.

No doubt they have told you numerous times that they will change – but have they at all since?

They are who they are, and your relationship will never improve to the state that you deserve. Their entire mindset and approach to relationships and you is not to build something – it's to win, dominate, and control. No ifs, ands, or buts. No rationalizing their actions. It's abuse even if they haven't harmed you physically.

Once you realize that truth, leaving is one step easier.

All change is difficult... but not necessarily negative. You will probably feel grief, anxiety, panic, loneliness, and desperation, but you need to learn to trust yourself and the series of emotions that led to your needing to leave.

Is the negativity at all related to your abuser personally, or is it just about the circumstances you would find yourself in? It's almost always the latter.

Five. How to Deal With Your Abuser

There are a number of techniques that are very useful in dealing with your abuser. They mostly center around directness, not avoiding confrontation, and being radically honest with yourself and your perception.

First, you must accept no excuses from your abuser. This includes excuses that you yourself generate for them.

You know that they never accept responsibility, and they pawn their shortcomings onto other people and things. This allows them to never be at fault, which places the blame constantly on you.

But resolving any problem and dealing with it first needs the recognition that they have made an error. Yes, it may have been circumstantial and other people were involved, but your abuser still made the choice to act, and you must force them to own up to it.

Make sure that you call them out on their actions, objectively and with examples, otherwise you will always be caught in their excuses. Carry a notebook around with you to document specific examples. You may even record their conversations between the two of you to play back to them.

Simply spell out what you did and what they did in objective, detached terms to try to highlight their actions.

This next part is of utmost importance: do not make excuses for them. Do not justify or rationalize their actions for them. Allow them to do that.

Don't feel compelled to break the discomfort and awkward silence by saying "Well, I know you didn't mean it…" or "I don't know, maybe I'm crazy and had a long day." This is you losing your steel over a couple of seconds of tension. Don't do it!

Second, you must judge them by their actions only, with little regard for their intentions.

Anyone can say that they're just trying to do good, but that doesn't mean they are actually doing it.

I can say that I was trying to rescue a cat by shooting it, but just because my intentions are good doesn't mean the act wasn't vile, ignorant, and reckless.

Your abuser will tell you time and time again that their intentions are pure and innocent, if not downright altruistic and "for your own good." But at some point, two things occur. (1) It just doesn't matter anymore given the poor treatment, and (2) you realize that they are lying to you about their intentions.

A pattern of poor treatment means that intentions are probably not positive. Let their actions speak louder than words and truly demonstrate how they regard you.

Ask yourself if you would accept this kind of treatment from a friend or a family member. The answer is probably a resounding "no" so why would you accept it from someone who purports to hold you in the highest regard?

Don't think about the alternate explanations you could conjure up for their actions. Face the harsh truth that their love for you may not be what it seems. How might their actions appear under that assumption?

As the saying goes, "fool me once, shame on you, but fool me twice, shame on *me*."

Third, set objective limits on what you'll accept *before* the fact.

If you set your limits during or after the fact, those limits will inevitably be skewed by your emotional investment in the situation and your abuser. Set your personal limits and dealbreakers beforehand so you can evaluate what state your relationship is in. If your abuser crosses the line, and perhaps your limits, you'll know exactly how little regard they have for you.

Hold these lines because your abuser has the singular goal of pushing your limits and getting away with as much as they can. This is because they know you have very weak boundaries.

They might argue that your limits are subjective, so root them in objectivity as much as possible.

Ask them if their mother, sister, or female friends would accept such behavior. Would he/she be embarrassed to speak to you or treat you the same way in public as he/she does private? They are obviously aware of objective limits and boundaries and just choose to ignore them.

For example, many of us have a hard boundary of being physically struck – being physically abused is a deal-breaker, and objectively so. We can define that beforehand. But in the heat of the moment, you might be able to explain it away due to explosive emotion and passion.

Don't let your confused attachment shift your rightful boundaries.

Fourth, only accept direct responses.

Don't allow them to keep dancing around issues, deflecting, and avoiding responsibility.

For once, tell them to cut the sugarcoating and actually answer your questions and concerns directly. Confront and call them out on this, and tell them that you know exactly how they are avoiding and deflecting. This takes practice with uncomfortable confrontation. You have to manage the tension and resist filling it with a justification for their behavior.

They'll likely defend themselves or attempt to confuse you by blaming you for something else. This is a tactic that they are using to escape answering you directly.

You might ask him why he keeps making fun of you in front of his friends. He might answer that he's just joking and that you need to loosen up. Keep asking why he does it when he knows or should know that it makes you feel terrible.

The focus is on how you feel, not how he feels, what he wants, or anything else. In a healthy relationship, a problem is listened to intently, fault is assigned, and real solutions are provided.

When you keep digging, you'll notice a pattern that they start getting upset at you and turning the conversation to how sensitive you are. This is not a direct response.

Repetition might be your best friend here.

Finally, be honest with yourself.

Only you truly know how you feel about your relationship, when all the excuses and eternal judgment are stripped away.

Are you actually happy in this relationship? Is it bringing you more pain than joy? Do you always feel like you are being judged, or putdown by your abuser and partner? Are you constantly afraid of losing them? Are they actually looking out for your well-being? Do you feel respected and loved by them? Finally, do you really think that they respect and love you?

Would you escape your relationship if you knew that you could, without any repercussions, judgment, sunk costs, or further abuse?

Is your fear of leaving based on a positive attachment to them, or a lack of self-esteem and security?

None of these are easy courses of action, but they are necessary in varying degrees in truly dealing with your manipulators and abusers.

Six. How to Disarm Your Abuser

This is a chapter dedicating solely to disarming and attacking back at your emotional abuser.

Let's do a quick recap on what makes your abuser tick. They are motivated by pure self-gain and accomplishing their goals. If they want to achieve something, they will stop at nothing to get it, and this includes manipulating and hurting people to do it. They won't feel remorse or regret while doing it, and can discard people as easily as a screwdriver that is broken.

Abusers don't react to you or your concerns because they don't care about them. They just want to make themselves happy by whatever means possible, and it's okay if that means pushing your head below water so they have breathing room. It doesn't matter if they have to make you cry, emotionally manipulate you, or rile you up on purpose. They'll get what they want.

Notice the pattern that they control you and get what they want through their handling of your emotions. In other words, they create specific emotional reactions in you intentionally to get what they want. That's their currency and their greatest power over you, because they simply don't care to be kind or decent.

If you can manage to react unemotionally, at least externally, that is the key to dealing with and disarming your abuser. Your emotions are what fuel their power. Without being able to affect your emotions, they will realize that you aren't buying their manipulation and become flustered at their tactics not working. They are at a loss for what to do.

First of all, don't react emotionally on an external level.

Stifle your reactions. Practice keeping a poker face. If you need to cry or sob, don't do it in front of them at the very least. Once they sense that they had found your weakness, they will keep exploiting it, so you can't show them so easily. If they know what pushes your buttons or makes you react, they will note that for later use as well.

In a similar vein, only say or reply with what is necessary. Don't voice opinions or thoughts, just keep your answers as short as possible. Your abuser is depending on you to show a chink in your armor and twist your words in some way. When you say only what is necessary and as little as possible, you deny them this chance and they will have much less ammunition against you. Of course, their new ammunition will be to say that you are being withholding and silent, but that is easier to rebut than an emotional outburst.

Be as short as possible and try to keep a stiff upper lip. Remember, you can emote as much as possible when you aren't face-to-face with them.

Second, generally focus on them more in conversation.

Get them to talk about themselves by asking question after question. Flip everything back to them. Ask how they feel about things and what they want to achieve.

What is the purpose of this point?

The abuser studies and learns about you. That's how they take advantage of your emotions. They're smart enough to know what your buttons are and how to set them off. They know you inside and out – because that's how they accomplish their goals through you.

Never talk about your feelings, inner thoughts, insecurities, and what makes you feel vulnerable. Reveal as little as possible and focus on them.

Talk about shallow topics like the weather, television, and your favorite type of coffee. Make your abuser feel like they have nothing to gain from it. They're not going to keep engaging with you if they can't learn anything they can use against you at some point.

They are like detectives trying to compile a case against you. Turn the tables and try to collect and obtain information about them that can possibly be used against them. Abusers will definitely have dirty skeletons in their closet that they are trying to hide – not out of shame, but because of how it reflects badly on them and how that will detract them from reaching their goals.

Third, get better with saying "no."

There's no way around it. You simply have to get better and more comfortable with confrontation and tension. That's part of what has enabled manipulative behavior – because you allow it to happen without strong enough objections.

Emotional manipulators are used to getting their way. They don't like being told "no" and probably don't hear it much. In fact, they might not even understand the concept of a boundary or a hard "no," viewing everything as flexible and negotiable. It's just a hurdle they can massage into a "fine, then". They've done it in the past, so they have learned to not listen to people refusing them.

It's a heavy burden but you might have to be the first to introduce them to the concept of "NO!"

You might have to do it multiple times in multiple ways, but simply adhering to "no" is something you get into the habit of. When an abuser hears the word "no" enough it is likely that they will simply stop and move on, and will probe to find the next weakness. They can be efficient in a cruel and ruthless manner.

Fourth, you need to adjust your expectations.

You're only useful to them when you can make them feel good. Keep this in mind, because it should influence how you approach them. If you can give them something positive or make them feel superior and intelligent, patronize them a little bit and that will go a long way towards how poorly they will treat you.

In other words, if you can tell them how smart they are, they will be subtly conditioned to treat you better because you've given them exactly what they are seeking.

The relationship isn't about support, pleasing them, or sharing. It's about you making them feel good about themselves. Change the goal posts and adjust accordingly.

Fifth, frame anything that you want in terms of how they would benefit from it, and how it would make people like them more.

Abusers want what they want.

If what you want conflicts directly or indirectly with that, it's going to be an easy choice because they don't want to compromise or humor you. Therefore, you must be able to spin and sell things to them in a way that makes them feel good about it.

Essentially, you have to make them feel like it would be a win for them too. You can do this with your needs as well – instead of making it about you, make it about them and how fulfilling or satisfying a need of yours would benefit their life. Stating your needs clearly won't work, and getting angry definitely won't either.

Once you speak to what benefits them, you're speaking their language and ironically on the same page. You can even remove yourself from your request and make it about all the ways that they will benefit in the present and future. If you want to go to a family dinner, you would talk about how much your family likes them, for example.

You are stroking their ego, making your needs a clear priority and win-win situation for them, and not dealing with their refusal to understand or care about your needs.

Sixth, get what you want upfront and don't rely on promises.

Don't give abusers credit, the benefit of the doubt, or your trust. Why?

Because they will violate it and never come through for you. Once they get what they want, it's on to the next thing, leaving you holding the short end of the stick. It's the ultimate one-sided deal – they will promise you the world in return for something, and once they receive it, they'll go into hiding and never pay like a shady gambler.

Most of the time, they will make promises and bargains they don't intend to ever keep. Sometimes, they just forget about upholding their end because they place zero to little priority on you. Whatever the case is, do not bargain with a narcissist without getting something immediately in return, and never rely on them to come through for you.

Finally, emotional abusers are driven by the need to obscure their insecurities.

They are deathly afraid of being exposed, and that other people will confirm their worst fears.

They have a deep fear of shame because that feeds their self-esteem and ego. They need to look good in front of others, they can never be wrong, and they need to be seen as a superlative.

They might not mind exposing their dark side to one person, you, but if the circle extends beyond you, that's when they start to get uncomfortable and filter their actions and words.

Simply ask them what other people would think, and allude to the fact that you will be talking to a host of other people about this, including people that they know or mutual friends. This will spark some action out of them.

They will frantically tell you that you should keep matters private and between just the two of you, but that's a false dichotomy. You absolutely have the right to simply ask your friends and family about your issues and life. You are not prohibited from airing your dirty laundry with others as long as it isn't a falsehood – and it certainly isn't.

They know it's not false, and that's why they would seek to prohibit you from doing it. They are acutely aware of what they are doing to you, and they worry about the judgment from others once they hear the truth.

In a relationship, the abuser controls the spin entirely. They control the narrative and what the future holds. But when they lose control of the spin and narrative, they fear their entire world crashing down on them, and most importantly, people thinking they are a bad person.

You're not. Don't ever think that.

Conclusion

I truly hope that this book has helped you shed light on the underhanded and covert emotional manipulation maneuvers that your abuser will use on you.

You should be able to see definitively that your abuser is not acting in your best interest or out of love. Well, it's love, but it's not love for you. It's a love of controlling and possessing you and for themselves.

I wish you the best on your journey.

Love,

Pam

Made in the USA
Middletown, DE
23 June 2017